JOHN KASICH is RUNNING for PRESIDENT!

A 2016 Presidential Election Coloring Book

Cover by Smerdloff
ISBN 978-1522793007

I0420272

John Kasich is running for President.

He wants to live in the White House.

John Kasich lives in
Columbus, Ohio, with
his wife, Karen Waldbillig,
and their two daughters,
Emma and Reese.

Kasich was
born in
McKees Rocks,
Pennsylvania,
a small town
near Pittsburgh,
on May 13, 1952.

Kasich is the son of
Anne and John, who was a mail carrier.

Both of his parents were the
children of immigrants
(Anne, the daughter of Croatians,
and John, the son of Czechs).

Kasich attended the Ohio State University.

As a freshman, he wrote an admiring letter to President Richard Nixon. Kasich was granted a twenty-minute meeting with the President in December, 1970!

At the age of 26, Kasich was elected
to the Ohio State Senate--
the youngest ever.

His first act as Senator was to
refuse a pay raise.

In 1982, John Kasich was elected to the U. S. House of Representatives, representing the district that includes Columbus, Ohio.

He was re-elected 8 times.

In the House, Kasich worked closely on the budget. In 1993, as ranking Republican on the House Budget Committee, he proposed an alternative budget with dramatic spending cuts, that was narrowly defeated.

In 1995, he became chairman of the House Budget Committee. And in 1997 he was the chief architect of the nation's first balanced budget since 1969.

In 1993, he created
his own alternative
to the Clinton
healthcare plan.

TIME Magazine reported that it would have "covered all Americans by 2005, using a form of an individual mandate that would have required employees to purchase insurance through their employers."

In 1996, Kasich introduced a welfare reform bill, the Personal Responsibility and Work Opportunity Act, which President Bill Clinton eventually signed into law. The Act limited the amount of time a citizen could spend on welfare, required work of welfare recipients, and provided child care credits intended to help move people from welfare to work.

After Kasich left Congress, he hosted shows on Fox News....

...then joined Lehman Brothers,
an investment banking firm,
where he remained until
the firm's 2008 collapse
at the start of the financial crisis.

Kasich was elected Governor of Ohio in 2010, and re-elected in 2014.

As governor, he:

*stripped funding from Planned Parenthood and signed legislation mandating additional procedures for women seeking an abortion

*has cut taxes (eliminating an estate tax, reducing an income tax) while raising sales taxes.

*eliminated a $6 billion budget deficit.

*accepted Federal funds from the Affordable Care Act to expand Medicaid in Ohio, to cover nearly 275,000 additional Ohioans.

"My mother used
to say it's a sin not
to help people who need
help, but equally a sin to
continue to help people who
need to learn how to help themselves."

November 8th, 2016, is Election Day.

Will America choose

John Kasich?

Draw YOU as President!

www.ingramcontent.com/pod-product-compliance
Lightning Source LLC
Chambersburg PA
CBHW081138280526
45787CB00007B/3130